DISASTER! FAMINES

By Dennis Brindell Fradin

CHILDRENS PRESS ®
CHICAGO

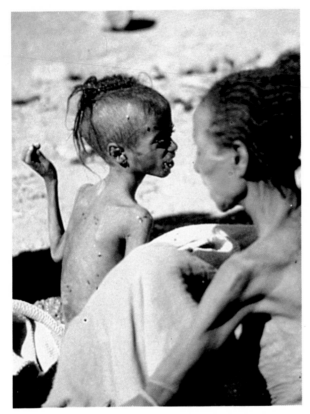

*Millions of people die
of starvation every
year. Experts say
some African
countries may lose an
entire generation to
starvation.*

Library of Congress Cataloging-in-Publication Data

Fradin, Dennis B.
　Famines.

　(Disaster !)
　Summary: Discusses the worst of disasters, famine,
focusing on that problem in several African countries
in the 1980s and mentioning some major famines in history,
such as China's in the 1870s, Ireland's of mid-nineteenth
century, and Russia's of the 1920s.
　I.　Title.　II.　Series: Fradin, Dennis B. Disaster!
HC79.F3F73　1986　　　363.8'2　　　85-31847
ISBN 0-516-00859-5

TABLE OF CONTENTS

1/ Ethiopia and Other
   African Nations— 1980. . . 5

2/ Witnesses: Africa, The 1980s . . . 11

3/ Causes and Effects of Famine . . . 27

4/ Some Major Famines . . . 35

5/ Predicting and
   Preventing Famines . . . 49

Glossary . . . 63

Index . . . 64

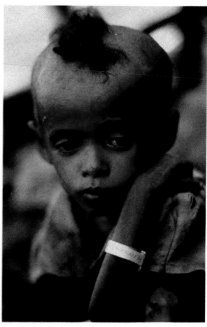

Relief worker (above left) feeds a child, in Mali, West Africa. A young famine victim (above right) shows off the identification bracelet which lists her name and the date of her arrival at the camp.

This mother and her baby are among the famine victims being cared for at Bati relief center in Ethiopia.

1/ETHIOPIA AND OTHER AFRICAN NATIONS—1980s

When I went there [to several African countries, in early 1985] I saw people digging in anthills to get pieces of grain away from the ants, and people feeding their hungry children leaves off trees.

—Cecil Cole, International Communications Officer, World Relief

In the fall of 1984 the world learned that hundreds of thousands of Africans had died in what was already one of this century's worst disasters. The killer was not an earthquake, flood, or any other spectacular and sudden assault of nature. In fact, the cause was a lack of something rather than a thing itself. By October of 1984 hundreds of thousands of Africans had died in a *famine,* a serious and prolonged shortage of food. The most distressing part of this news was that more than 150 million more people were threatened as the famine continued.

Some of the causes of the famine were natural while others were man-made. Even during the best of times Africa is a poor continent. It depends on farm products for the survival of most of its half-billion people. For several years the rainfall throughout much of Africa had been far lower than usual, causing crops to wither on the stalk and livestock to die of thirst. This left millions of persons in more than two dozen countries with little or nothing to eat.

Drought has turned this once-green land into a barren wasteland. Death is a grim reality in Africa.

War was one of the man-made causes of the famine. As of late 1984, Ethiopia, Mozambique, Chad, and several other African countries were engaged in civil wars. In certain areas of these war-torn nations supply routes were cut off and people couldn't move about in search of aid. War also meant that a large portion of the male population was engaged in killing rather than in saving lives.

Poor planning on the part of several African governments worsened the situation. The most glaring example of this was in Ethiopia, where in late 1984 the government was spending $200 million to celebrate the tenth anniversary of its coming to power. This celebration, centered in the relatively well-fed capital city of Addis Ababa, took place while thousands of rural Ethiopians were dying of hunger in the parched fields of the north.

The international community was also guilty of a poor response. Relief organizations had warned throughout 1983 and 1984 that the food situation in some African countries was deteriorating. Little attention was paid to these warnings until October, 1984, when a British Broadcasting Corporation report on Ethiopia was shown on worldwide TV. Only when people saw the rows of emaciated corpses did they realize what was happening in Africa.

This feeding center feeds hundreds of Ethiopians everyday.

Relief workers who arrived in Africa in November, 1984 were faced with a horrendous situation. In Ethiopia, at least 300,000 persons had died from the combination of malnutrition and disease. Famine had also claimed as many as 200,000 lives in Mozambique, and thousands more had died in Senegal, Chad, Mali, and Sudan. Help was desperately needed for the more than 150 million others whose lives were threatened.

To save these people, food was needed—millions of tons of it. Within a few days of the television broadcast, the United Nations approved $416 million for emergency food assistance to Ethiopia and several other African nations. At the same time the United States committed $45 million for food aid to Ethiopia, while the European Community allotted $42 million for aid to Ethiopia, Chad, Niger, Mali, and Mauritania. Around the world, individuals donated money to such relief organizations as the Red Cross, Oxfam America, CARE, and UNICEF, which were sending aid to the stricken nations.

By November planeloads of food and medicines were regularly arriving in Addis Ababa, the capital city of Ethiopia, which was the country receiving the most aid. Relief workers found that getting the food to Ethiopia was just half the battle. Rural people were the ones most in need of food, and most of them lived more than twenty miles from a road. To make matters worse, there were just six thousand trucks in all of Ethiopia, and all but a few hundred of these were being used by the military to fight a civil war.

The airplane cargoes were loaded onto the available trucks and then driven to rural food camps set up by organizations such as the Red Cross and UNICEF. As word spread that food had arrived, hordes of people headed for the camps, often walking several hundred miles to get there.

At some of the feeding centers there were so many people and so little food that medical personnel and relief workers had to decide who would live and who would die. Persons who seemed to have the best possibilities of survival were marked with crosses on their foreheads and then fed, while those near death were left to starve.

Another problem in the camps was a lack of medicine. Many persons had been so weakened by hunger that they easily succumbed to influenza, measles, and other diseases. Lacking the proper drugs, doctors in some camps could do little more than watch the sick persons die.

By early 1985 the tremendous amount of aid to Ethiopia was showing results. People still were starving, but the death rate had fallen from hundreds to just twenty or so per day. Despite the increased food supply, the continuing drought meant that the survivors still couldn't grow their own crops. The influx of food, medicine, and other aid would have to continue for a year or more.

The unfortunate part of the focus on Ethiopia was that other famine-stricken African countries didn't receive

A UNICEF convoy (above) rushes medical supplies to relief camps. Dead and dying famine victims (left) lie outside the Bati intensive care unit in Ethiopia.

enough attention. Although the situation improved in Ethiopia, it worsened in such countries as Chad, Sudan, and Mali.

In Chad, which had several million hungry people, a "wall" of about 100,000 persons encircled the capital city of N'Djamena in hope of obtaining food. Feeding centers were established to help these and other hungry Chadians, but by early 1985 one thousand people per month were dying of malnutrition and disease in Chad. In Sudan, the country to the west of Ethiopia, more than a million people were in danger of starving to death in spring 1985. In Mali a sixteen-year drought had made the situation so bad that farm families were devouring their seeds. This meant they would have nothing to plant even if the rains came.

As of spring 1985, more than 1.5 million Africans had died in the famine and hundreds more were dying each day. Even with no end in sight, this disaster already ranked as the deadliest famine ever recorded in Africa.

Ethiopian children who reach the food camps are the lucky ones.

2/WITNESSES: AFRICA, THE 1980s

Those who have experienced a disaster—either as victims or witnesses—have the best understanding of its impact on people. During the African famine of the 1980s hundreds of relief workers from around the world worked day and night to help feed and care for the victims. Here are the stories of three such people.

Herb Snedden: Ethiopia

In mid-February, 1985, Herb Snedden, an official with the disaster-aid organization World Relief, left his family in Atlanta, Georgia, and flew to the city of Amsterdam, in The Netherlands. There Snedden helped supervise the loading of 83,000 pounds of food, medical supplies, and equipment onto a transport plane. Snedden and several other persons then boarded the plane and headed for Addis Ababa, Ethiopia, about 3,500 miles away.

This U.S. army raft carries 36 truck loads or 15,000 tons of food per day across Mali's Niger River.

One of the most difficult aspects of relief work is making certain that the aid gets to the needy people. During many disasters, relief materials have fallen into the hands of thieves or ended up rotting on some pier or runway. World Relief had assigned to Snedden the job of seeing to it that the supplies reached those who needed them.

Flying with Snedden were two other relief workers. One was a representative of the General Baptist Conference, an American organization that had provided the bulk of the supplies along with World Relief and World Relief Holland. The other person was a private citizen from Orange County, California, who wanted to make certain that the two well-drilling rigs she was taking to Ethiopia were put to the proper use.

After a short stop in Cairo, Egypt, the plane arrived in Addis Ababa early on the morning of February 14, 1985. "At the airport three other transports besides ours had just landed and were unloading," Herb Snedden recalled, several months after his Ethiopia trip. "One was from the Red Cross, the second from Save the Children, and the third I can't remember. We had hired two trucks and it took them about six trips to unload the goods from our plane and take them to the building where we stored them.''

Some of the goods were distributed in Addis Ababa to representatives of needy people. The two well-drilling rigs were also left in Addis Ababa under the stipulation that people from rural areas could borrow them to dig for water. The remainder of the materials were then taken by truck to famine-stricken areas in the north.

"First we went with a truckload of goods to a northern rural area where a feeding station was to open,'' continued Snedden. ''Most of Ethiopia is mountainous and the roads through the mountains were the roughest I've ever been on. What would have been a three-hour trip on a highway in the United States turned out to be a two-day trip.

"As we drove we saw hundreds of people streaming in from the northeastern province of Wallo, which was very hard hit. These people looked extremely malnourished, extremely desperate. They were walking towards Addis Ababa a couple of hundred miles from their homes in hope of getting food.

"The feeding station we were delivering the food to wasn't supposed to open for a week, but people had heard about us coming and were waiting for us. I spoke to some of the people through a translator. What they were concerned about most was their children—about food and medical attention for them. They thanked me because they understood we had brought the supply of food. I'm sure some of those I saw are dead now, but even in that state many of them were ashamed that they had to subsist by what they considered handouts from foreigners. All of the people were farmers, and some of

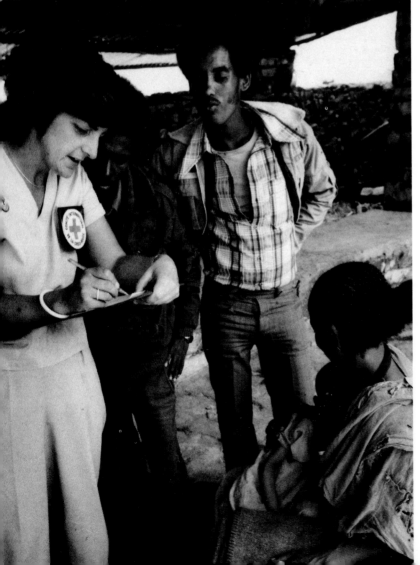

A young British Red-Cross worker (above) aids famine victims at the Bati camp. A New Zealand volunteer nurse (left), working with the International Red-Cross, checks on the health of a child at vitamin and blanket distribution center.

The feeding program at Bati can feed 500 children at a single sitting. This child is waiting for his daily meal. Thousands of children are fed like this everyday.

them hadn't been able to grow a thing for three years because they hadn't had any rain in that time."

Snedden made a second trip to another feeding station in northern Ethiopia. Two weeks after his arrival in Ethiopia he had completed his job, and so he returned by airplane to Atlanta, Georgia.

More than seven thousand miles from Ethiopia and several months after his return, Herb Snedden thought back on the journey. "My fear is that a lot of the aid to Ethiopia is going to dry up because the situation has improved somewhat. When people saw pictures of starving children there was a tremendous response, but now that the death rate has gone down people may think there's no longer a problem. Even if the drought ends and rain begins to fall, the feeding still will have to go on until early 1986 because it will be that time before the food situation will improve within the country.

"I'm also worried that people who contributed to provide food for Ethiopia won't be so eager to provide money for development within the country." Snedden pointed out that in order to avoid future famines Ethiopia needs help in developing programs on scientific farming, well digging, reforestation, and soil conservation.

"Scientific farming is a much less emotional topic than starving children, but it is just such programs that can prevent starvation in the future," Herb Snedden concluded.

Rudy von Bernuth: Ethiopia

In early November, 1984, Rudy von Bernuth, an official with the relief organization CARE, flew to Addis Ababa. His objective was to survey the situation and decide how CARE, a private relief agency based in New York City, could best help.

Von Bernuth spent three or four days meeting with people involved in emergency activities and also with officials of the Ethiopian government. Together they decided that, since the northern part of the country was receiving a great amount of assistance, CARE could do the most good by helping in another area.

"We determined that a place that had the warning signs of getting just as bad as the north was Hararge Province in the eastern part of Ethiopia, right along the borders of the countries Somalia and Djibouti," explained von Bernuth. "This region includes major portions of the Ogoden Desert, which is occupied by nomadic people and farmers who

16

Opposite page: Rudy von Bernuth, a CARE worker, was in charge of relief programs in Thailand before he was sent to deal with the famine crisis in Ethiopia.

Bags of wheat from CARE (above) lay in front of an emergency food distribution site in Hararge Province. Over 900,000 people in this region have been affected by the drought. CARE provided emergency food to 250,000 people that will gather at government centers, such as the one shown below.

depend on rain-fed agriculture. Before making the final decision to concentrate on this region, we decided that we should visit it.''

Rudy von Bernuth flew from Addis Ababa to the town of Dire Dawa in eastern Ethiopia, where he again met with government officials. As is his habit when he visits a famine-stricken area, von Bernuth also went off alone to speak to the people about what was happening.

"I spoke to the leader of one clan and asked him how long they had been at that site,'' continued von Bernuth. ''He said a month and a half and told me that eleven children had died during that time. Another indication of the seriousness of the situation was the large number of men around. Among nomadic people the men are usually out herding cattle. They weren't doing that because the cattle had died. I could also see that the people were suffering from severe malnutrition.

''I was convinced that the people of Hararge Province would be dying in droves if something weren't done soon. I then returned to Addis and spent a couple days working up a proposal to the Ethiopian government to provide food for 250,000 persons in the area we had visited, and to bring in personnel to monitor the food distribution.''

Before leaving Ethiopia, von Bernuth spent some time touring other areas of the country. In northern Ethiopia he visited the huge refugee camp at the town of Korem.

''There were roughly thirty thousand people—many of them sitting out in an open field with no shelter whatsoever— at the Korem camp,'' continued von Bernuth. ''The lack of food is rarely the immediate cause of death in a famine. The immediate cause is usually a disease such as pneumonia or measles, which a healthy person would recover from, but which hungry people succumb to because they are in a

Drought destroys the farmers' livelihood. It kills the crops, and, without food and water, the cattle die. More than 18,000 people in Korem, Wollo Province (below) have to withstand near-freezing, nighttime temperatures without proper shelter in order to be near food stations.

weakened state. It was easy to see how diseases could claim the lives of those people who were sitting outside all night with no place to go and little clothing.

"I got up the morning after arriving at Korem at 6:00 A.M., just as the light was coming over the horizon. . .and went to the mortuary. I saw the people who had died during the night being prepared for burial. Mothers were wailing, old men were reading from the Bible, and there were little family groups scattered about. While I was there the death rate at Korem was astronomical—about 50 people per day—and yet that was down from the 100 or 120 per day which had been occurring there several weeks earlier.

"From the mortuary I went into the hospital area where thousands of people were crowded together in six or seven metal buildings that resembled old airplane hangars. The hospitals didn't have regular beds. The beds were raised mounds of earth with stones around the edge. There were

Famine victims lie on stretchers at Korem. In spite of the efforts of a few dedicated Ethiopian and foreign doctors and nurses, thousands have died of measles, bronchitis, pneumonia, and other common diseases made deadly by the famine.

At shelters run by volunteer doctors and nurses the staff can only care for the worst cases. Young children suffering from severe diarrhoea have a chance to live if they receive medical attention.

some dedicated Ethiopian and European doctors there, but very few to handle the several thousand sick people who were crowded into those sheds. After three days in that area I returned to the United States.

"As I flew back from Ethiopia to America the image that stayed with me was the helplessness of the small children," concluded von Bernuth. "I kept comparing their plight with the relatively well-off condition of the children in America, including my own nine-year-old daughter. I was thinking that all children should have as good a life as most children have in America."

Within a few weeks of Rudy von Bernuth's visit to Ethiopia, more than forty-thousand tons of food were on the way from CARE to the Hararge Province. In addition, CARE purchased a fleet of trucks to distribute the food and also sent relief workers and health workers into the province to help the people. These efforts helped this area of Ethiopia avoid the high death tolls suffered by other regions of the country.

Kristina Schellinski
is an information
officer for UNICEF.

Kristina Schellinski: Kenya, Uganda, and Sudan

"Informed people knew what was happening in Africa long before aid was mobilized," said Kristina Schellinski, an information officer specializing in the African emergency for UNICEF. "The information was available that it hadn't rained, that the crops had died, and that there was a severe food shortage. Yet until the BBC film in October of 1984 there was no willingness on the part of the developed countries to help with the problem of African hunger."

UNICEF (the United Nations Children's Fund) was one organization that was aware of the developing African famine situation at an early stage. In June 1984 the organization sent Schellinski on a fact-finding tour of Kenya and Uganda — countries not far from having severe famine conditions.

"When I arrived in Kenya I went into the northwest part of the country in the Lake Rudolf region where the Masai people were gathered. The land was dry and barren and there were several lakes you could drive right through because all the water had dried up from them. Everything was the same earthen color — cattle, shrubs, and people — as if a blanket of

Kristina Schellinski's photographs of famine victims were taken in the Sudan, at a camp close to the Ethiopian border.

brownish dirt covered the countryside. Although many of the people I saw were malnourished at that time, the government of Kenya had not declared that there was a food problem. I could see that unless some actions were taken there would be large numbers of severely malnourished and even starving people in the country.''

From Kenya, Schellinski went to Uganda, the country to the west. ''When I arrived in Kampala, Uganda's capital, I found it hard to believe that the country had a food shortage because there was a lot of lush vegetation around the city. But when I drove northward I could see the withered fields of corn, the dusty fields, and the malnourished people.''

Schellinski went into northeastern Uganda where she visited a feeding center operated by UNICEF. ''The most disheartening thing was that they had run out of supplies at this center. People had walked long distances there to get help, but when they arrived there was nothing.

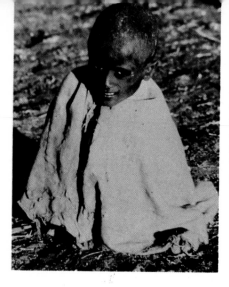

According to Kristina Schellinski, "Orphans [such as the one shown at left] have a very low chance of surviving without someone watching especially over them."

"I met a family who had walked four or five days to get there. They told me they had once had oxen and cattle but that they had all died or been sold to buy food. They had planted seeds repeatedly and lost them because of lack of rain. These people had finally been forced to eat the last hope they had—their seeds. Many people had done this, but what often happened was that they got awfully sick because the seeds had been chemically treated to resist drought. Finally, this family had run out of everything. They had four children and they were all very malnourished. A fifth child had already died."

This particular family was saved because the doctor serving as Schellinski's interpreter admitted them to a hospital. There they received food as well as treatment for tuberculosis. "It's good to help people on a single basis like that, but what is needed most is a large-scale program for helping multitudes of people," explained Schellinski.

Kenya and Uganda averted the horrendous famines that Ethiopia, Mozambique, and other African countries suffered. This was partly because the drought in Kenya and Uganda was not as severe as in other African lands, and, partly because the people of those two nations received aid in time. But then in January, 1985 Kristina Schellinski went to Sudan, a country then experiencing a terrible famine. In Sudan she visited three camps—two of which were populated by Ethiopian refugees and one where Sudanese people were gathered.

"I found people terribly sick and starving in all three camps in Sudan. I remember there was an eerie silence over the shabby huts and tents that stretched for miles. You didn't even hear children crying because when you are starving the natural response is to keep quiet and conserve body energy. The only sounds you could hear were people coughing from TB [tuberculosis] or whooping cough.

"I'd walk past the hospital—which was just a couple of wooden poles covered with woven mats made of leaves—and inside there'd be people lying on the floor covered by blankets. You wouldn't even see individual faces because there were three or four people huddled under one blanket."

Because UNICEF is concerned with children, Schellinski observed the young people in the camps very closely. "Among the Ethiopian refugees there were a number of children whose parents had died during the trek into Sudan. The children had just followed the stream of people into Sudan. There are very few relief workers in the camps and I'm afraid those orphans have a low chance of surviving without someone watching especially over them."

Care for orphaned children is just one ongoing need that countries such as Ethiopia and Sudan will have long after the famine is over. Schellinski pointed out that famine survivors need assistance with health and nutrition problems over a long period of time.

"You must realize that even when there is no special famine going on, 15 million of the world's children die annually as a result of the combination of malnutrition and disease, and that in Africa alone 5 million children die each year from these causes. UNICEF considers it crucial to address not only the problem of famines but also the terrible death toll during these so-called normal circumstances."

UNICEF has estimated that 15 million children die each year from malnutrition and disease. The Cambodian children (left) are suffering from malnutrition, blood poisoning, and malaria. Their suffering is primarily caused by the civil war in Southeast Asia.

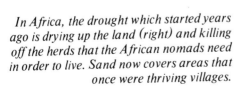

In Africa, the drought which started years ago is drying up the land (right) and killing off the herds that the African nomads need in order to live. Sand now covers areas that once were thriving villages.

3/CAUSES AND EFFECTS OF FAMINE

. . .Hunger is as old as history. The world literally lives from hand to mouth, never more than one crop away from hunger. . . .

— *Will There Be Enough Food?*
U.S. Department of Agriculture 1981 Yearbook

A Hungry World

It is difficult to determine how many hungry people there are in the world, because poorer countries don't keep accurate records. According to the lowest estimates, about 15 percent of the world's people are malnourished even when no large-scale famines are going on. According to the highest estimates, the figure is closer to 67 percent, or two thirds of the world's people. Whatever the true percentage, it can be said with certainty that hunger is an ordinary part of life for more than half a billion people. Although the poorer nations have more hunger, no nation is completely free from the problem. In the United States, which is one of the wealthiest nations, at least several million people either don't get enough food or can't obtain the kinds of foods the human body requires.

The result of all this hunger is a tremendous amount of misery and death. Each year many millions of persons around the world die from diseases resulting from malnutrition, with children suffering the most deaths. In the poorest countries

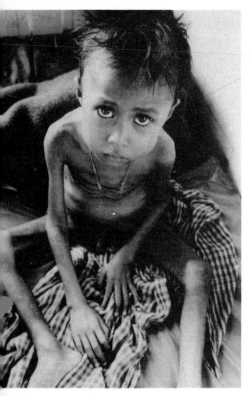

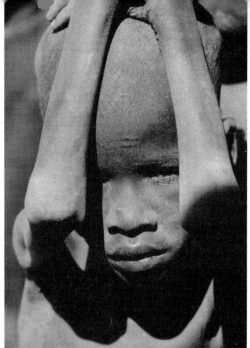

More lives have been claimed by famine than have been lost in all the hurricanes, tornadoes, earthquakes, volcanic eruptions, floods, and fires that have ever occurred on earth. The Cambodian boy at left died. We do not know the fate of the African boy shown above.

malnutrition kills up to 50 percent of the children before they reach the age of five. Worldwide, UNICEF has determined that 15 million children die annually as a result of malnutrition and disease. In the countries where most of these childhood deaths occur, the populace as a whole may live to an average age of just forty or forty-five, as opposed to the average of more than seventy in the wealthier nations.

The Deadliest Disasters of All

In countries where many of the people are hungry even during ordinary times, all it takes is a minor drought or political upheaval to create a terrible famine. When this happens, the death toll can be unbelievably high. For example, in late 1984 a million Ethiopians died from hunger and disease within three months. Had that death rate been maintained, every last person among Ethiopia's population of 35 million would have perished within nine years.

The fact is that famines are the very worst of all the disasters that befall humanity. More lives have been claimed by famine than have been lost in all of our planet's hurricanes, tornadoes, earthquakes, volcanoes, floods, and fires combined. Even if all the deaths from every war ever fought were added together, the total wouldn't nearly equal the number of lives claimed by famine.

The deadliest famine ever recorded was probably one in northeastern China between 1876 and 1879. The death toll in this disaster—as many as 13 million—was nearly equal to the number of people who died in battle during all of World War II. Many other times famine has killed millions of people. For example, a horrendous famine in India in 1865-67 claimed possibly 10 million lives, and one in the Ukraine region of the Soviet Union killed an estimated 5 million persons in 1932-34.

The countries most vulnerable to famine are those that are poor, highly populated, and large. A poor nation with a large population usually has difficulty producing enough food for its people even during normal times, and is usually just one crop failure away from famine. The governments of large countries often have difficulty reaching all their people during times of crisis. The three nations that have suffered the most from famines—China, India, and Russia—are highly populated and large and have also been poor throughout most of their histories.

Causes of Famine

The four leading causes of famine are drought, flooding, plant diseases, and war. Of these, drought (a prolonged period when rainfall is well below normal) is by far the leading cause.

People have deserted this drought-stricken village in Mauritania. In order to solve Africa's long-term problems, many complex political and environmental situations must be changed.

Farmers move into a region because it has adequate rainfall for growing crops and raising livestock. Although that area may have plentiful rainfall for many years, there may come a time when the rainfall suddenly falls off and the crops wither. This is drought.

Entire civilizations have been destroyed by drought-caused famines. About 4,500 years ago one of the first great early civilizations developed in the Indus River valley. Two of this civilization's main cities were Mohenjo-daro and Harappa, both located in present-day Pakistan. This civilization faded in about 1700 B.C., possibly due to drought-caused famines. Droughts were also probably a major cause of the end of the Cliff Dweller civilization in what is now the southwestern United States around the year 1300.

If a drought covers a large enough area and goes on long enough, a country that was once green can turn into a desert and death tolls can reach astounding proportions. A three-year drought caused the horrendous famine that killed up to 13 million Chinese persons in 1876-79. Drought, too, was the major cause of the ongoing African famine of the 1980s.

Some regions are more drought-prone than others. For example, areas that receive barely enough water for farming even in ordinary times don't need much of a drop in rainfall to experience drought. The Great Plains of the United States is such a region, but fortunately the U.S. is wealthy enough to prevent famine despite the droughts. Africa's Sahel region is another dry area prone to drought. The Sahel—covering parts of Mauritania, Senegal, Mali, Niger, Chad, and several other countries—experienced a drought-caused famine during the late 1960s and early 1970s that claimed about a million lives.

Although a lack of rainfall is the primary cause of famine, too much water can also destroy the food crops. China has suffered hundreds of famines due to floods of its Yellow River, which has been nicknamed "China's Sorrow." In 1889 as many as 2 million persons died in the flooding and subsequent famine along the Yellow River, and in 1929 and 1930 a famine caused by more flooding of this river claimed another 2 million lives. Hurricanes (also called *typhoons* and *tropical cyclones*) have caused famines by flooding crops under many feet of water.

Just as people are subject to disease, so are plants and animals. Plant diseases often have wiped out crops, causing severe food shortages. The most famous example of this occurred in Ireland during the 1840s, when a fungus destroyed much of the country's potato crop, the main food for most of the Irish. The ensuing famine claimed a million lives. Diseases in livestock herds have also contributed to famine conditions.

Probably the most tragic famines of all are the ones brought about by war, because these are the most avoidable. Wartime conditions were responsible for a famine in India in 1943-44 that cost more than 1.5 million lives. Incredibly, governments have even used famine as a weapon during wartime. During the civil war in Nigeria between 1967 and 1970, the Nigerian government blockaded food supplies headed for the rebels in the region called Biafra. The resulting famine claimed more than a million lives.

Effects of Famine

No matter what the cause, the effects of famine are always tragically similar. A famine-stricken area is a place of hunger, sickness, misery, and death.

Food is a necessity of life, providing us with energy and the materials to maintain and repair our bodies. After going without eating for a day or so, a person starts to feel weak and his or her body begins using its reserve food supply. As the reserve food is used up, the weakness intensifies until finally, after six weeks or so, the person dies. Death almost always results by the time the person has slipped to about 60 percent of his or her usual body weight. This means that a 150-pound adult can't survive with a weight much below 90 pounds. Because they are growing, children can't go as long as adults without eating. The elderly also suffer rapidly from lack of food, because they generally are not in as good condition as young and middle-aged adults.

As Rudy von Bernuth pointed out, the immediate cause of death in a famine is usually disease rather than starvation. Persons weakened by lack of food are extremely vulnerable to various illnesses. What makes disease even more of a threat during a famine is that thousands of people may be crowded

Their swollen bellies tell doctors that these children are suffering from a disease called kwashiorkor.

together in unsanitary conditions as they await food. This creates the possibility of a large-scale outbreak of disease called an *epidemic*. Among the diseases that commonly take many lives during famines are influenza, typhus, measles, cholera, and dysentery. Another terrible disease often suffered by young famine victims is called *kwashiorkor* (a word from the African country of Ghana meaning "deprived child"). Kwashiorkor is a protein deficiency that bloats children's stomachs and leaves them weak and susceptible to other diseases.

One awful effect of famine does not show up in the statistics: permanent brain damage in children. A child who has a long-term lack of nutritional foods can suffer brain damage that will be a lifelong problem even if he or she receives proper food later on. Children who lack the proper foods also tend to be small and more delicate than the rest of the population. This makes them prone to illness and other physical problems as adults.

It is important to remember that death tolls express just part of the story. Those fortunate enough to survive famines often suffer from mental and physical problems for the rest of their lives.

A mother carries her children from the flooded home in Dacca, Bangladesh. Over 1,200 persons died and millions were left homeless in this 1974 flood.

4/SOME MAJOR FAMINES

And there was a famine in the land: and Abram went down into Egypt to sojourn there; for the famine was grievous in the land.

—The Bible, Genesis 12:10

Famines have plagued humankind for longer than history has been written. One of the earliest references to famine was found on a carved stone slab in an ancient Egyptian tomb. The inscription contains these heartbreaking words of an Egyptian pharaoh who lived more than four thousand years ago:

I am mourning on my high throne for this vast misfortune because the Nile flood in my time has not come for seven years. Light is the grain and there is a lack of crops and of all kinds of food. Each man has become a thief to his neighbor. . . .The child cries, the youth creeps along, and the heads of the old men are bowed down. . . .Torn open are the chests of provisions but instead of contents there is air. Everything is exhausted.

Famine has made so deep an impression upon the human mind that the holy books of many peoples contain references to these disasters, which were often viewed as punishments sent from God. The Bible, for example, contains at least twenty references to famine.

Because famine-prone regions tend to have poor communication with the rest of the world, very little is known about many of the deadliest of these disasters. Also, many of the worst famines occurred centuries ago in places where few persons could read or write. The following famines, therefore, aren't necessarily the worst that ever occurred, but they are ones about which something is known.

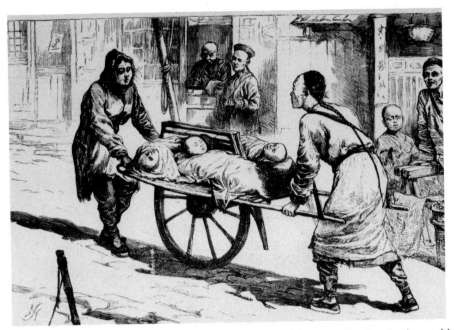

Throughout its history, China has endured some of the worst famines in the world. This 1877 illustration shows mothers selling their children in order to get food.

China 1876-79

China, the most populous nation on the earth, has suffered many of the worst disasters. An earthquake that shook China in 1556 claimed more than 800,000 lives, making that the deadliest earthquake ever recorded. A flood of the Yellow River in 1887 claimed at least 900,000 lives, making that the deadliest known flood. However, the very worst disasters ever to strike China have been famines.

According to a Chinese university study, nearly two thousand famines took place in China between about 100 B.C. and A.D. 1900. This means that the country experienced an average of about one famine per year during that period. A famine in the years 1333-37 is thought to have claimed more than 4 million lives. As bad as that was, an even worse famine occurred in northeastern China between 1876 and 1879.

Because of its lush farmland, the northeastern part of China is sometimes called the "Garden of China." However, between 1876 and 1879 very little rain fell in this region, and wheat, millet, and sorghum crops died. Soon people in a huge area covering 300,000 square miles were suffering from famine.

At the time China had very poor communications. Large numbers of people had died by the time officials in the capital city of Peking learned of the famine. Because of the country's poor roads, the government had trouble transporting relief supplies to the stricken people. One of the most tragic aspects of this famine was that food sat rotting in port cities while the Chinese government tried to figure out a way to take it to the starving populace.

The food was finally placed on carts, but little of it reached the villages. Famished people attacked the carts and sometimes killed each other fighting over the food. So desperate did the people become that some resorted to eating human flesh, as described in this report written in 1876:

Hungry mobs stripped cloth from corpses, robbed merchants and raided homes in search of money to buy grain. In the market place, children and women were sold for [money]. In time, families were forced to break up and search for food independently. Starving children were often killed by desperate parents who subsequently took their own lives. Roving packs of hungry dogs and wolves not only ate the flesh of the dead but attacked the living as well. The most shocking consequence of famine was the rapid spread of cannibalism. At first the people ate only the rotting flesh of the dead. But later they began butchering the living. Despite strict governmental injunctions, human flesh was sold openly in the markets.

By 1877 people were dying in such large numbers from hunger and disease that they were buried in mass graves still called "ten-thousand-man-holes." By the time the famine ended in 1879, between 9 and 13 million Chinese persons had died, making this probably the deadliest famine ever.

Street kitchens (below) were all that kept many Indians from starvation during the famine of 1943. A triple line of starving Indians (above) slowly moves towards a soup kitchen in Calcutta. Some of these people died before they could reach the food. In this famine more than 1.5 million Indians died of starvation and disease.

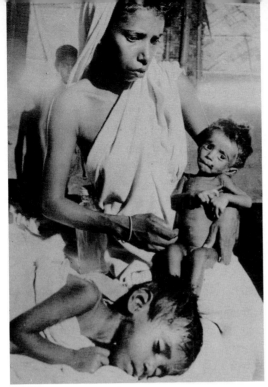

A mother cradles her infant son as another sleeps at "Save the Children" hospital in an Indian refugee camp. In 1971, this mother faced starvation, along with some sixty million other refugees, because of the floods that had raged through East Pakistan and the West Bengal region of India.

Famines in India

India's great leader Mohandas Gandhi once said, "If God should appear to an Indian villager it would be in the shape of a loaf of bread." After China, India is the nation that has suffered the most famine deaths. On some lists, five of the ten deadliest famines of all time occurred in India. Many times the country has suffered more than a million famine deaths within a single year.

One of the most common causes of famine in India is the failure of the *monsoons.* These are spring and summer winds that pick up moisture from the Indian Ocean and drop it as rain on India and other countries of southern Asia. The failure of the monsoons means that rain doesn't fall, which in turn means that crops don't grow. Gigantic storms called *typhoons* also have destroyed crops in India, resulting in famine.

Human factors, too, have played a tragic role in creating famines in India, a crowded nation with an ever-growing

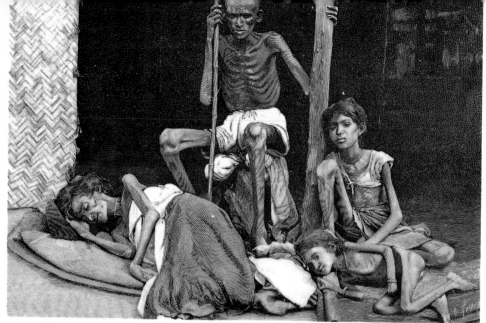

An artist captures the desperation and hopelessness of an Indian family starving to death because of drought and famine.

In 1958 this woman left her village searching for food. More than 450,000 people were hungry because the once rich, rice-producing region had endured a drought that had lasted for five years.

population. Many times invaders have seized large quantities of food in India, resulting in the starvation of large numbers of Indian people. In past centuries Indian lawmakers were also known to destroy growing crops in order to starve out invaders, depriving many of their own people of food in the process. During one such famine in the early 1600s it was recorded that "the number of the dead exceeded all computation or estimate. The towns and their environs and the country were strewed with human skulls and bones."

When the British took control of India in the mid-1750s, the famine situation grew even worse. Under British policies the price of food was raised, and rural people often could not afford it. From the time of the British takeover until very recently, India suffered a major famine every five years or so. One of the worst occurred in 1865-67 in the eastern part of the country.

In 1865 the monsoon rains failed in eastern India, causing large-scale hunger in the state of Orissa and neighboring regions. Great Britain could easily have sent food to the stricken people. But the British governors decided to export the extra food produced in India's other regions to countries that could pay for it.

By 1867, when millions of people had already died and millions more were in peril, the British finally decided to send in food. However, in a tragic turn of events roads were washed out by torrential rains, which kept supplies from getting through. The result of all this bad luck, poor planning, and inhumanity was that as many as 10 million persons died in Orissa and neighboring states.

India has experienced many other terrible famines within the last century or so. From 1876 to 1878, at the time when drought was killing crops and people in China, a failure of the monsoons brought about a famine that took 5 million lives in India. In an even more recent tragedy, a famine caused mainly by wartime conditions claimed at least 1.5 million lives in India's Calcutta region in 1943-44.

Ireland's Great Potato Famine of 1846-51

For more than seven hundred years, from the late 1100s until the early 1900s, England ruled the island of Ireland. For most of that time the English treated the Irish people like slaves and kept them poor and uneducated.

By the 1840s more than half of the 8 million Irish people lived in tiny huts and ate little or nothing else besides potatoes. As long as the potato crop was plentiful, the people could at least survive. But then, between 1845 and 1847, a fungus disease destroyed much of Ireland's potato crop. By 1846 large numbers of people were starving to death and dying of disease.

To make things even worse, the winter of 1846-47 was an extremely cold one. During that winter, a man named N. M. Cummins of Cork described conditions in the town of Skibbereen, but his description would have been true for much of Ireland:

> . . . Six famished and ghastly skeletons, to all appearance dead, were huddled in a corner on some filthy straw, their sole covering what seemed a ragged horse-cloth. . . .I . . .found by a low moaning, they were alive. . . .The same morning the police opened a house on the adjoining lands . . .and two frozen corpses were found lying upon the mud floor.

England made little attempt to assist Ireland, which was just one of its numerous colonies at the time. In fact, some English landlords threw Irish tenants out of their huts because they could not pay the rent. The evicted people were left to live in ditches and along dirt roads, where many perished.

On the humanitarian side, relief workers came from England, the United States, and other countries to help the Irish people. They set up soup kitchens in parts of the Emerald Isle, but unfortunately they didn't have nearly enough food to go around.

Those who could afford to leave Ireland boarded ships and sailed away from their starving homeland. The Irish called the vessels on which they sailed "coffin ships," because thousands of starving and sick emigrants died on the overseas

42

When disease caused the potatoes to rot in the fields, famine hit the Irish farmers. Before it ended more than a million men, women, and children (left) died of starvation and disease. The population of Ireland which had stood at eight million before the famine, was reduced to 5.5 million by 1851.

voyages. Thousands of others arrived in the United States, Canada, England, and Australia, where their descendants live today.

The potato blight finally came to an end in the late 1840s and the deaths tapered off. By the time the Great Potato Famine ended in 1851 approximately 1 million Irish people had died and more than a million others had left the country. Because of the "Great Hunger," as this disaster is sometimes called, Ireland's population dropped from 8 million in the early 1840s to just 5.5 million in 1851. Mainly because of the Great Hunger, Ireland's population today is only about half of what it was in 1845.

The Russian Famine of 1921-22

Russia, the largest country in the world, has suffered from more than a hundred major famines since the 900s A.D. One of the worst occurred in 1921-22 in southern Russia's Volga River valley, usually one of the most fertile and productive regions of the country.

War set the stage for this disaster. Between 1914 and 1920 Russia's agricultural production had dwindled because of World War I and a civil war. Food was scarce as the 1920s

This was one of the first tractors to be used on a Russian collective in 1929. Before technology was introduced the Russian farmers used only human and animal labor.

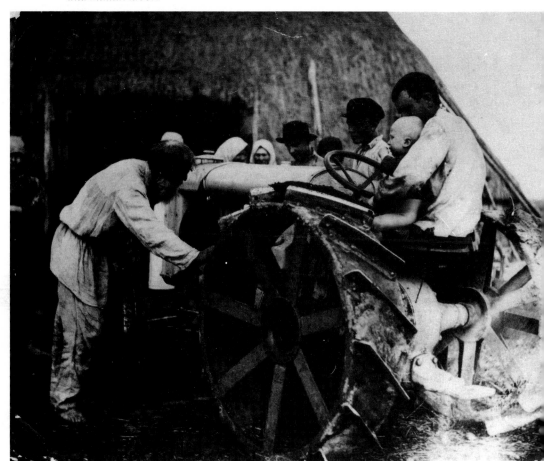

Before the Revolution of 1917, only the few — the aristocracy — had land and money. Most Russians were landless and poor. When drought or war disturbed the balance of nature, starvation for the poor was inevitable.

began. To make matters worse, the Volga River valley received inadequate rainfall in 1920 and the next year the rains failed completely. By late summer of 1921 a million square miles of farmland resembled a desert and 30 million persons were suffering from hunger.

The Russian government and outside relief agencies brought in food, but the afflicted region was so large that many people couldn't be reached in time. When Quaker relief workers entered the stricken area in September, 1921, they found that people were eating grass and making bread out of tree leaves, dirt, and water. Because growing children are the first ones afflicted by famine, the Russian government set up some special feeding homes for the young. But these were

Starving Russians at a soup kitchen in St. Petersburg

just crowded and filthy places of death, as is evident from this description by a Quaker relief worker:

> As a home it was intended for 50 children, but yesterday 654 children were crammed within its walls. . . .As we entered we became aware of the continual wailing sound that goes on day and night. In each room. . .there were at least a hundred children packed like sardines in canvas beds—six on a bed intended for one, and underneath the beds as well. The typhus cases, some of them completely naked, lay on straw in a separate room. They had neither bedding, medicines nor disinfectants, though we had been able to give them a little soap and clothing. They had no doctor.
>
> Each morning the attendants picked out the dead from the living and put them in a shed to await the dead cart which every day makes its round of the Children's Homes.

Because they didn't have enough food for all the hungry people, relief workers had to decide which persons to try to save and which to let die. As is usual during famines, some of the relief workers had to be talked out of giving their own food to those who had none. Had they done this they would have become sick themselves, leaving no one to care for the starving people.

By mid-1922 the relief workers had brought in enough food to save most of the remaining people, and by the time Russia enjoyed a good harvest in 1923 the famine was over. It is estimated that 5 million persons may have died in this famine—more people than Russia had lost in World War I.

SOME MAJOR FAMINES

Date	Place	Estimated Deaths
1333-37	China	Probably more than 4 million
1769-70	India	Between 3 and 10 million
1846-51	Ireland	1 million
1865-67	India	As many as 10 million
1876-78	India	5 million
1876-79	China	Between 9 and 13 million
1889	China	2 million (in Yellow River floods and subsequent famine)
1892-94	China	Nearly a million
1896-97	India	5 million
1899-1900	India	More than 1 million
1921-22	Russia	Up to 5 million
1928-29	China	3 million
1929-30	China	2 million (famine caused by Yellow River flooding)
1932-34	Russia's Ukraine	5 million
1943-44	India	More than 1.5 million
Late 1960s-early 1970s	Sahel nations of Africa	About 1 million
1967-70	Biafra in Nigeria	More than 1 million
Beginning in 1984	Much of Africa	More than 1.5 million

In order to avoid famines in the future, work must be done now. Introduction of new disease-resistant crops, such as rice in the Philippines (above) and experimental sorghum plants (left) will increase the amount of food that can be grown.

5/PREDICTING AND PREVENTING FAMINES

Two Averted Famines

Several times in recent years famine has been averted thanks to adequate warnings and quick action. One such success story occurred in 1967.

Bihar is a state in northeastern India that has been devastated by drought-related famines many times. One of the worst famines to strike the Bihar region killed up to 10 million persons in 1769-70. During the mid-1960s the Bihar region was again struck by a drought that turned thousands of square miles of farmland into desert. Once more it appeared that famine would claim hundreds of thousands of lives in this part of India.

However, the government of India and several international relief organizations were aware of the crisis. By the spring of 1967 they had alerted the world about it. The world's response was to send a tremendous amount of food and other aid to the Bihar region.

The United States, which provided 9 million tons of wheat, sent in more food than any other nation. Relief organizations such as CARE, UNICEF, and Oxfam also brought in tremendous quantities of food, and the government of India provided medicines so that outbreaks of disease could be avoided. Indian radio stations continually broadcast information about where people could go for food and medicine, and a special effort was made to provide extra food for growing children.

Civil war caused ten million refugees to flee to the cities. Despite relief efforts, in many slum areas children fought with animals for garbage.

As a result, a situation that had threatened to claim millions of lives actually killed very few people. The death rate in Bihar even dropped during this period, because many people had more food than usual thanks to the relief supplies.

Another success story just four years later involved India and the country of Bangladesh. This time war instead of drought was the cause of the threatened famine.

From 1947 to 1971 the country of Pakistan was divided into two parts, which lay on either side of India—East Pakistan and West Pakistan. Throughout the 1960s the people of East Pakistan grew dissatisfied with the way the Pakistani government was treating them. In March, 1971 they declared themselves free of Pakistan and announced that the name of their new country was Bangladesh. The Pakistani government sent thousands of soldiers to fight the rebels in Bangladesh. The clash between the two forces cost thousands of civilian lives.

In spring of 1971 people in the newborn country of Bangladesh began to cross over into India to avoid the bloodshed. By October of that year more than 9 million people had moved from Bangladesh to India. Many experts predicted that famine would claim millions of lives among the refugees, who had little more than the clothes on their backs.

What happened, however, was that the government of India, together with such agencies as UNICEF and Oxfam, provided food and other necessities for the refugees. In December, 1971 India joined the people of Bangladesh in their war against Pakistan. When the Pakistani army surrendered later that month, the relief camps in India were closed and the 9 million refugees from Bangladesh returned home. Thanks to the government of India and the relief agencies, famine once again had been averted.

Predicting Famines

Ideally, every potential famine would have the same happy ending as the ones in India in 1967 and 1971. It doesn't seem right that the human race, which has walked on the moon and conquered most diseases, should allow even a single person to die for lack of food. And yet in 1984 alone more than a *million* persons died in the African famine within a few months.

Predicting famine is the first step toward saving people. By 1967 the government of India had worked out effective ways of determining when a famine would occur. India is an old country and has learned to deal with famines over several thousand years. But many other nations in Asia, Africa, and South and Central America have no methods for gathering information on impending famines.

This doesn't mean that the world is totally unaware of potential famines in these countries. Several United Nations

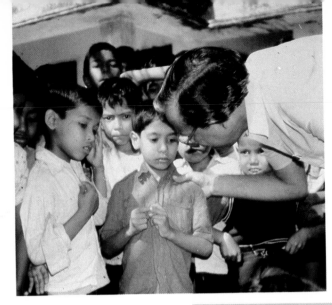

Relief workers throughout the world rush to help the needy. Paul Munshi (left), a World Relief director, visits an orphanage in Khulna, Bangladesh.

World Relief has built irrigation projects in India (right).

UNICEF also brings technological improvements to third world countries. The young African child (left) is drinking clean water from a pumping system built by UNICEF.

agencies report on conditions that may cause famines in poor countries. Relief organizations such as the International Red Cross and CARE also employ workers who report on impending famines. However, there is no effective and sufficiently funded program to quickly spread the news about a potential famine. A tragic proof of this is that it took a TV news crew to alert the world of the recent African famine, by which time the situation was out of control.

Relief workers say that millions of lives could be saved each decade if there were a good early-warning system for famines. Such a famine-predicting system could be run by a special branch of the United Nations.

Weather monitoring would be an important part of this system. Satellites and airplanes could provide data about droughts and other weather conditions that cause famines. The famine-predicting network would also include experts to provide information on agricultural, political, and social problems in famine-prone nations.

Ideally, an international agency for predicting famines would identify potential famine areas and spread this information throughout the world via newspapers, TV, and radio. Gathering and dispersing information about a potential famine is just the first step for averting disaster, however. The crucial step is to quickly bring in huge quantities of food— often millions of tons—to the stricken region.

One of humanity's main goals should be to provide that food when it is needed. Unfortunately, this is extemely costly. The United Nations doesn't have the billions of dollars necessary to assist in every famine crisis in the world. The United States and other developed nations can't even feed all their own people, let alone those people who face famine elsewhere.

There is another difficulty in assisting people every time there is a food crisis. Countries that have famines tend to have them again and again. This means that, unless the conditions leading to famines are changed, food may have to be brought in to those countries every few years.

Preventing Famines

Most experts believe that the best way to attack the famine problem is to alter the conditions in famine-prone countries. Many kinds of changes are needed.

- *Reducing Population Growth.* In the year 1900, about 1.5 billion people lived on the earth. By 1960 the figure had doubled to about 3 billion. By 1983 the total had reached 4.7 billion. Some experts think that by the year 2025 our planet will be home to 10 billion people. This steady increase of population in an already hungry world is so dangerous that some people have called it the "population bomb."

The population is growing most rapidly in the poorest nations. Such countries face the risk of deadlier famines with each passing year.

By slowing their rates of population growth, poorer nations could reduce the deaths from famine. The best way to achieve this is for the people of these countries to plan smaller families—two or three children instead of five or more. The governments of many of these countries have tried to convince their people to do this.

These efforts began to pay off in the mid-1980s when, for the first time ever, global population growth began to slow. If this trend continues, humanity may be able to avoid the horrendous famines that might otherwise be our destiny.

When drought, famine, or flood hit any country, the children suffer the most. Experimental schools, such as the one in Mauritania (left), and school milk programs, such as the one shown in Honduras (right), bring hope for the future generations.

• *Helping Children during Normal Times.* The millions of children who live on the edge of starvation even during normal times are those most vulnerable to famine. They are usually in such poor physical condition that they cannot survive a food shortage for very long.

Several organizations are continually engaged in helping these children. One measure promoted by UNICEF and other organizations is the breast-feeding of infants in poorer countries. Not only is mother's milk more nutritious and less expensive than bottled milk, but it also provides children with immunity to disease. Another important ongoing project in many countries is *immunization*—protecting people from disease with vaccines. It costs just a few dollars to immunize a child against many common diseases, and it can be a lifesaving measure. A number of relief organizations also provide children in poor countries with foods and nourishing liquids to help them maintain good health.

Irrigation project in India

These programs not only help children survive during famines, but also reduce children's deaths during normal times. In fact, UNICEF estimates that half of the 15 million children who die annually from malnutrition and disease could be saved from such measures as breast-feeding, immunization, and oral rehydration (the providing of liquids to protect children from dehydration due to diarrhea).

• *More Irrigation Projects.* Even when no rain falls, water can be brought to thirsty farmland through irrigation. In a typical irrigation project, a river is dammed to create a large lake called a reservoir. The water then flows from the reservoir to dry farmland through canals. The digging of wells to tap water deep in the ground is also an important kind of irrigation.

During the past twenty years irrigation projects have allowed farmers in many drought-ridden countries to grow plentiful crops. For example, drought-caused famines are not the problems that they once were in China, India, and Russia partly because of recent irrigation projects. Many more

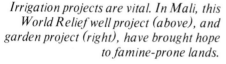

*Irrigation projects are vital. In Mali, this
World Relief well project (above), and
garden project (right), have brought hope
to famine-prone lands.*

irrigation projects need to be constructed in the near future to
help the world's farmers in their battle against drought.

• *Improving Farming Methods.* Farmers in developed
nations have tractors and other machines to help them with
their work. In poor nations, however, many farmers still
depend on ox-drawn plows and human labor, just as their
ancestors did five thousand years ago. One reason these
farmers have large families is that they need lots of hands to
help with the work.

In recent years farmers in the poorer countries have been
acquiring farm machinery — often with the help of their
governments and assistance agencies. This machinery helps
produce the larger crops which help prevent famines.

The use of improved seeds is an even cheaper way to assist
farmers in famine-prone lands. Scientists are continually

A young girl roams through newly planted seeded trees in Senegal. Plants prevent soil erosion.

developing seeds that produce faster-growing and larger crops. The UN's Food and Agriculture Organization (FAO) and other relief agencies are supplying these improved seeds to farmers in famine-prone nations, thereby helping them to increase their productivity.

• *Soil Conservation.* In countries that depend on farming, soil is as valuable as gold—and just as difficult to replace if it is lost. During droughts, windstorms can pick up all the topsoil from a region and blow it away. Considering that it takes roughtly a hundred years to create each inch of topsoil, a single windstorm can destroy a thousand years of nature's work. And yet in many drought-prone countries little effort is made to conserve that valuable soil.

One major problem is that too many forests have been cut down in some of these countries. Trees are extremely important in drought-prone lands because they soak up rainfall, hold down the soil, block the winds that whisk away valuable topsoil, and provide shade. Throughout history countries that have cut down too much of their woodlands have suffered because of it. For example, during the 1930s a drought in the central United States was made worse because trees and other vegetation that held down the soil had been cleared too extensively. Forests being planted today in many drought-prone countries will help with soil conservation in the future.

Farmers in these regions are also being taught scientific farming methods for conserving soil. One of these methods is *contour plowing*, which involves plowing the soil and planting crops *across* rather than *up* slopes. Contour plowing helps fields hold rainfall better. The planting of *cover crops* to enrich the soil and hold it down is another conservation method that the world's farmers are learning.

A Need for Changing Attitudes

Humanity has never been free of hunger and famine. These problems will probably always be with us to some degree despite programs developed to combat them. The big question is: What are we going to do about the hundreds of thousands of people who die each year from lack of food?

Inside Philadelphia's John F. Kennedy Stadium, on July 13, 1985, as fans patiently waited for the start of the Live Aid Concert

Some of the most popular singers in the U.S.A. recorded "We Are The World," and raised millions of dollars to help African famine victims.

A change in attitude could help the situation immediately. Workers in Africa in 1984-85 have pointed out that people give large sums of money when they see pictures of starving children, but are less eager to contribute to irrigation and farmer-education projects. These programs are less dramatic than starving children, yet they are the very things that can prevent famines.

The media might also devote more attention to famines developing in far-off lands. Had the recent African famine been reported earlier via newspapers, TV, and radio, hundreds of thousands of lives might have been saved.

Finally, if nations could find a way to exist peacefully with each other, there would be far less hunger in the world. Hundreds of billions of dollars are spent each year on building bombs and weapons—far more than is spent on assisting the hungry. Wouldn't it be better to spend that money on all those millions of starving people?

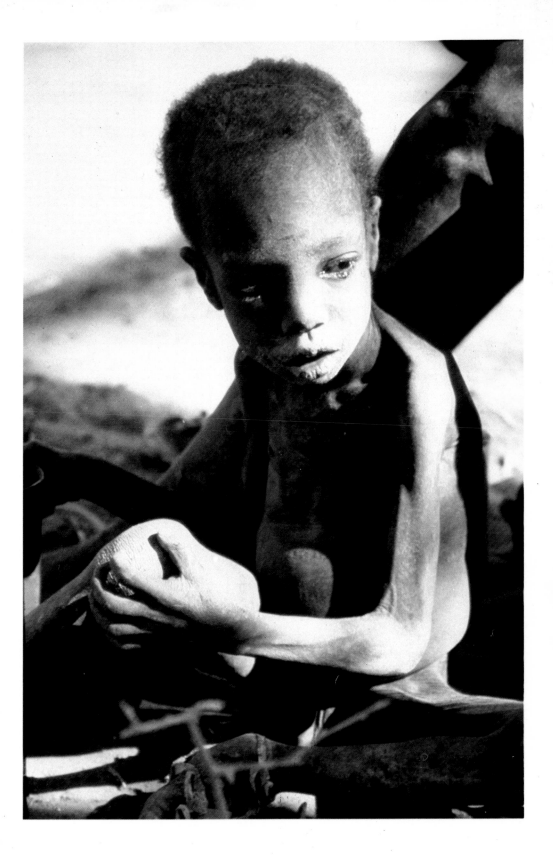

Glossary

Blight   a fungus disease of plants

Cannibalism   the act of humans eating human flesh

Desert   an arid area—usually sand—in which little or no vegetation will thrive

Disease   an illness or sickness in an animal or plant

Drought   a long-term absence of rain

Famine   the extreme lack of food, leading to starvation

Fertile   capable of producing or reproducing; fruitful

Irrigation   the system of furnishing water for agriculture by ditches or canals

Malnutrition   the condition caused by insufficient bodily nourishment

Mobilize   to prepare for war or a specialized service

Pestilence   any infectious disease, such as plague or cholera, that spreads quickly

Reforestation   the planting of trees in areas where they have been removed or destroyed

Soil conservation   the system of methods used to maintain the top soil in the best condition for growing things

Starvation   the state of extreme hunger

Technology   the scientific methods used to produce the desired products or conditions

Top Soil   the top layer of soil—usually the most fertile

Index

Page numbers in boldface type indicate illustrations

Addis Ababa, Ethiopia, 6, 7, 11, 12, 13, 16, 18
Africa, 5-25, 31, 60
Amsterdam, The Netherlands, 11
Atlanta, Georgia, 11, 15
attitudes toward famines, changing, 59, 60
Australia, 43
averted famines, 49-51
Bangladesh, 50, 51, 52
Bati relief center, Ethiopia, 4, 9, 14
Biafra, 32
Bible, 35
Bihar, India, 49, 50
brain damage, 33
British Broadcasting Corporation, 6
Cairo, Egypt, 12
Calcutta, India, 41
Cambodia, **26**
Canada, 43
cannibalism, 37
CARE, 7, 16, 17, 21, 49, 53
causes of famine, 29-32
Chad, 6, 7, 9, 31
chart: major famines, 47
children, help in normal times, 55, 56

children, sold by mothers, **36**
China, 29, 31, 36, 37, 41, 56
"China's Sorrow," 31
Cliff Dwellers, 30
"coffin ships," 42
Cole, Cecil, 5
contour plowing, 59
Cork, Ireland, 42
cover crops, 59
Cummins, N.M., 42
deaths, from famines, 7, 9, 20, 28, 29, 31, 32, 33, 36, 37, 39, 41, 43, 46, 47, 49
Dire Dawa, Ethiopia, 18
disasters, deadliest, 28, 29
diseases, 18, 20, 25, 27, 28, 32, 33, 55
Djibouti, 16
droughts, 8, 9, 29-31, 49, 58
earthquakes, 36
East Pakistan, 50
effects of famine, 32, 33
Egypt, 12, 35
England, 41-43
epidemics, 33
Ethiopia, 4, 6-9, **10**, 11-21, 24, 25, 28

European Community, 7
famines:
  in Africa, 5-25, 31, 60
  attitudes toward, changing, 59, 60
  averted famines, 49-51
  causes, 29-32
  in China, 29, 31, 36, 37, 41, 56
  definition of *famine*, 5
  disasters, deadliest, 28, 29
  effects of famines, 32, 33
  in India, 29, 32, 39-41, 49-51, 56
  in Ireland, 31, 41-43
  major famines (chart), 47
  predicting famines, 51-54
  prehistoric famines, 35
  preventing famines, 54-59
  in Russia, 29, 44-46, 56
  world hunger, 27, 28
famine victims, **2, 4, 6, 7, 10, 14, 15, 19, 20, 21, 23, 24, 26, 28, 33, 34, 38, 39, 40, 43, 46, 50**
farming, improving, 57, 58
flooding, 29, 31, 36
Food and Agriculture Organization (FAO), 58
Gandhi, Mohandas K., 39
General Baptist Conference, 12
Ghana, 33
Great Britain, 41
"Great Hunger," 43
Great Plains, United States, 31
Hararge Province, Ethiopia, 16, **17**, 18, 21
Harappa, 30
Honduras, 55
hurricanes, 31
immunization, 55
India, 29, 32, **38, 39**, 39-41, 49-51, **52,** 56, **56**
Indian Ocean, 39
Indus River valley, 30
Ireland, 31, 41-43, **43**
irrigation, 56, **56, 57**
John F. Kennedy Stadium, Philadelphia, **59**
Kampala, Uganda, 23
Kenya, 22, 23, 24
Khulna, Bangladesh, 52
Korem, Ethiopia, 18, **19, 20,** 20
kwashiorkor, 33
Live Aid Concert, **59**
major famines (chart), 47
Mali, 4, 7, 9, **12,** 31, **57**
malnutrition, 7, 23, 25, 27, 28
Masai people, 22
Mauritania, 7, **30,** 31, 55
medicine, 8
milk, mother's, 55
Mohenjo-daro, 30
monsoons, 39, 41
Mozambique, 6, 24
Munshi, Paul, **52**
N'Djamena, Chad, 9
Netherlands, The, 11
Niger, 7, 31

Nigeria, 32
Niger River, **12**
Ogoden Desert, 16
oral rehydration, 56
Orissa state, India, 41
Oxfam, 49, 51
Oxfam America, 7
Pakistan, 30, 50, 51
Peking, China, 37
Philadelphia, 59
Philippines, 48
plant diseases, 29, 31
population growth, reducing, 54
potato famine, 31, 41-43
predicting famines, 51-54
prehistorical famines, 35
preventing famines, 54-59
Quaker relief workers, 45, 46
rainfall, 5, 30, 39, 41, 45
Red Cross, 7, 8, 13, 14, 53
rice, disease-resistant, **48**
Rudolf, Lake, 22
Russia, 29, 44-46, 56
Russians, aristocracy and poor, **45**
Sahel region, Africa, 31
St. Petersburg, Russia, 46
Save the Children, 13
"Save the Children" hospital, **39**
Schellinski, Kristina, **22,** 22-25
schools, experimental, **55**
seeds, improved, 57, 58
Senegal, 7, 31, **58**
Skibbereen, Ireland, 42
Snedden, Herb, **11,** 11-13, 15
soil conservation, 58, 59
Somalia, 16
sorghum, disease-resistant, **48**
Soviet Union (*see* Russia)
Sudan, 7, 9, 23, 24, 25
Thailand, 17
topsoil, 58
tractor, Russian collective, **44**
trees, 58, **58**
tropical cyclones, 31
typhoons, 31, 39
Uganda, 22, 23, 24
Ukraine, 29
UNICEF, 7, 8, 9, 22, 23, 25, 28, 49, 51, 52, 55, 56
United Nations, 7, 51, 53, 58
United States of America, 7, 21, 27, 30, 31, 42, 43, 49, 53, 58
Volga River valley, 44, 45
Von Bernuth, Rudy, **16,** 16, 18, 20, 21, 32
Wallo Province, Ethiopia, 13
war, 6, 29, 31, 32, 41, 44, 50
"We Are The World" recording, **60**
West Pakistan, 50
world hunger, 27, 28
World Relief, 5, 11, 12, 52, 57
World Relief Holland, 12
World War I, 44, 46
Yellow river, 31, 36

Photo Credits

About the Author

Dennis Fradin attended Northwestern University on a partial creative writing scholarship and was graduated in 1967. He has published stories and articles in such places as *Ingenue, The Saturday Evening Post, Scholastic, Chicago, Oui,* and *National Humane Review.* His previous books include the Young People's Stories of Our States series for Childrens Press and *Bad Luck Tony* for Prentice-Hall. He is married and the father of three children.